SHINE!

SHINE!

Light for All People

An Advent Study for Adults

Patricia Farris

Abingdon Press
Nashville

SHINE!
LIGHT FOR ALL PEOPLE

Copyright © 2011 by Abingdon Press

Library of Congress Cataloging in Publication data has been requested.

ISBN: 978-1-426-71627-0

11 12 13 14 15 16 17 18 19 20—10 9 8 7 6 5 4 3 2 1

MANUFACTURED IN THE UNITED STATES OF AMERICA

Contents

Introduction

How we love this season! But is it here already? Another year past and time for a new church year to begin? Where has the time gone? Wasn't it just summer? Back-to-school? Halloween? Thanksgiving? Black Friday? Cyber Monday? Bam! The December days are rushing up on us like oncoming headlights on the freeway.

Wouldn't you much prefer for the light to shine around and within you instead? Do you long for light in the shadow places of your heart? Do you pray for the light of life to shine on all the hurting and broken places of this world? Do you yearn to live into a future brimming with the light of God's hope and peace?

Scripture assures us again and again that the light shines in the darkness. Indeed, the light of Christ shines healing, salvation, wholeness, and peace into the hurting places of our hearts and into the broken places of our world. It shines bright in the lives of all who trust its healing energy and its truth. It glows on the horizon of the future, heralding God's promised reign of righteousness and love for all people.

Perhaps the metaphor of light is less powerful now than it was way back in biblical times. For those of us who live in brightly lit houses and cities, it's easy to flick on a switch and send the darkness scampering away. Of course, not so many generations ago, before electricity and before gas lamps, city streets were dark at night. Homes were dark, too, save for the light of candles and oil lanterns. It was what historian William Manchester called "a world lit only by fire."

A small oil lamp was what my grandfather used as a boy on his southern Illinois farm. How many times, when I was a little girl, did he tell me the story of doing his homework by the light of the lamp that he still had on the table in his den? Then he'd turn off all of the lights, strike a match, and light the lamp. To my eyes, nothing was more magical, more beautiful, or more reassuring than seeing the warm glow of his old lamp light up the room. In darkness, there was light.

It's Advent. It's time again to light the lamps and the candles. It's time to hear the Word of God again, time to put our houses in order for all the festivities of Christmas. It's time to put our spiritual houses aright to be ready for the birth of the Christ Child. The Epistle speaks to us: "You will do well to be attentive to this as to a lamp shining in a dark place, until the day dawns and the morning star rises in your hearts" (2 Peter 1:19*b*).

I invite you to bring your minds and your hearts to this Advent adventure with Christ. What will God's best gift to us be this year? What new surprise will we discover? What will make the old, old story new for us? What will Advent's light reveal?

Week by week, may the season of Advent glow brighter and brighter in the light of God's love for you and for all people. Wait. Watch. Even now the light of Christ is coming into the world. Advent has begun.

—Patricia Farris

8

The Light in the Window

Where can I go from your spirit?
  Or where can I flee from your presence?
If I ascend to heaven,
    you are there;
    if I make my bed in Sheol, ‑(hell)
      you are there....
If I say, "Surely the darkness shall cover me,
    and the light around me become night,"
even the darkness is not dark to you;
    the night is as bright as the day,
    for darkness is as light to you.
                            Psalm 139:7-8, 11-12

In Week 1 of our Advent study, we will start when it's night inside our own hearts. And we will explore the places where we long for light to shine.

Is It Dark Yet?

One Christmas Eve, I was sitting in the congregation during the late-afternoon family service. The sanctuary was packed with eager children, slightly frazzled parents, and beaming grandparents. Sitting next to me was a little four-and-a half-year-old girl. She sang the carols, listened intently to the Christmas story, and prayed the Lord's Prayer out loud, along with all those worshiping around her, all with a minimal amount of squirming and giggling with her big brothers. But about forty minutes into it, she'd had about all the waiting she could muster.

She leaned over to me conspiratorially, little hand cupped around her mouth so that she could whisper something into my ear. "Is it dark yet?" she asked. "Is it dark yet?"

It took me a few moments to realize what she was really asking. Her question was not simply about the relative lightness or darkness of the night sky just outside the comforting glow of the church sanctuary. "Is it dark yet?" she asked again. Seeing that I clearly did not comprehend the full import of her question, she again leaned close to whisper in my ear.

"When we get home," she explained, "we get to open one present—but only after it's dark." "Oh," I said, smiling at her dad, who was sitting on the other side of her brothers on down our pew. "Well, it's *getting* dark," I said, carving out a bit of wiggle-room for her parents while hoping to underscore her sense of expectation and excitement. "Yes," I told her, "it's getting dark. Pretty soon, after you all get home, it will be getting dark."

What wise parents, who knew to measure time not by clocks but by the things children can see for themselves. Daytime. Nighttime. Light. Dark. Her parents were also teaching their children that even the darkness can hold the promise of something new, something wonderful, something special, a gift. These are the "treasures of darkness": greater knowledge of the wisdom and love of God to be found when the light around us becomes night (Isaiah 45:3).

When It's Very Dark

"Advent begins in darkness," the wonderful preacher Fleming Rutledge has said. For centuries, the church has set aside these four weeks of Advent as a time of spiritual deepening. The new church year begins with time for getting in touch with our own deep yearning for God and with our earnest longing for the light. If we receive it as such, the season of Advent is the church's gift of time set aside to visit the darkness in our hearts, the places of sorrow and hurt. This is the season the church has created for when it's very dark inside and the darkness seems almost too much to bear. The season of Advent can be for us a time to be honest with God and with ourselves. It can be a time to find new light for our path, for Advent marks the beginning of our annual walk toward the light of God (Isaiah 2:5).

We long for the light. It's there all the time, but can we slow down enough to perceive it? Just as it takes time for our eyes to adjust to the dark, our souls need time to recalibrate. We need to reset our inner clocks to allow for contemplation and prayer. The Advent wreath in many of our homes and churches is actually designed to do just that.

Do you know the history and the meanings of the Advent wreath? It comes from a custom older than the church itself. It is said to have begun in pre-Christian times. After the harvest was in and as the nights grew longer and colder, the people of northern Europe, those who worked the land and plowed the fields, would take one wheel off the wagon. They would lay the wheel down on its side. Work would stop. Instead, they would take time in the stillness and quiet of the very dark night sky to linger and look for the stars, to light candles and light up the darkness of the long night.

This is hardly the pace of Advent we experience, is it? Instead of stopping the wagon, as our ancestors would do, we ramp up to overdrive at this time of year, don't we? We make ourselves busier than ever during the lead-up to Christmas. There are presents to buy and cookies to bake, parties to plan, and relatives to receive. There are homes to decorate, school plays, parties, and cards to mail or e-mail. Even the church itself can become frenetically busy.

11

Watch out! More often than not, we turn this beautiful season, meant to be a time of reflection and preparation, into a harried and fatiguing cacophony of busy-ness. We light the candles one-by-one each week, but we scarcely pause to contemplate their message. It's up to us to choose to put some "advent" adventure back into Advent. The opportunity is ours; the choice is ours to make.

How will we find time to stop in order to begin anew? Where will we find space to pray? Might we give ourselves permission to take a wheel off the wagon of our fast-paced schedules and look deep into the darkness in anticipation of the light?

Where will we find the light? In her droll wit, in *Teaching a Stone to Talk: Expeditions and Encounters,* Annie Dillard puts it this way: "You do not have to sit outside in the dark. If, however, you want to look at the stars, you will find that darkness is necessary." We know this, but we forget; or we just don't want to be inconvenienced. Sometimes it takes "an act of God" to reveal the treasures of darkness to us.

Here's the story of one such act of God, to be sure. A few years ago, when the whole of Eastern Canada and the United States was plunged into darkness during a massive power outage, Jay Reynolds, the Director of the Walter R. Sheely Planetarium, near Cleveland, Ohio, described what that dark night came to be for him and for his neighbors. Before sunset, so that all of his neighbors could see what he was doing, Dr. Reynolds set up his telescope in his front yard, inviting everyone to come over and see the marvels of the sky once it got dark. That night, the deep, deep black of the sky free of artificial light revealed the galaxies in plain view. The whole sky was alive. The planet Mars was brilliant and the Perseid meteor shower as well. Dr. Reynolds said: "It was a great night to see the stars the way they were meant to be seen."

This perceptive astronomer loved the night sky so very much. He saw great opportunity when the total absence of electricity revealed a pitch-black sky. He knew that "treasures of darkness" would be revealed amidst what Galileo called the "starry messengers." What could have been a long night of fear became, instead, a serendipitous, joyful celebration, a time for fellowship, for learning and for joy.

I have no doubt that in the darkness of that night, those neighbors in Bay Village, Ohio, experienced opportunity where it hadn't seemed possible. In the darkness, they could reconnect with their Creator, who sets the stars in their courses and binds together Orion and the Pleiades. For the first time in ages, they could see the stars the way they were meant to be seen, and explore the treasures of darkness.

> *You, O LORD, keep my lamp burning;*
> *my God turns my darkness into light.*
> ### *Psalm 18:28 (NIV)*

But have we not all had nights of forgetting that the myriad stars are shining overhead in the dark night sky? Have we not wakened in the middle of the night, troubled by all the cares and worries of the day, which only seem to grow bigger and more fearsome in the dense darkness?

As grownups know all too well, the darkness holds not only treasures, but terrors. Sometimes it brings not gifts, but loss. Sometimes there are times of darkness in our lives that seem interminable, that hurt too much. As we embark together on this Advent study, among us will be those whose hearts are heavy and upon whom true sorrow lies like a blanket of grief.

Christmastime can be a season of increased anxiety and depression, when the darkness of the winter nights becomes the darkness of the soul ... where there is an empty chair at the table, a recent diagnosis of illness, treatment endured ... where there is loss and tragedy ... where there is not enough money to pay the bills let alone buy presents ... where a marriage is ending ... where downsizing means that your job is about to end ... where the best medication can't seem to quiet the internal demons ... where depression persists like the unwanted guest....

In every life will come times of painful defeat or loss; times of cruel disappointment and grief; times when this life seems very, very dark to us. There are times when life tastes bitter, times when sorrow crushes, times when all of the stars seem to have gone out and we fear that the dawn will never come. These are times when we feel like Job, invoked by President Obama after the tragic shooting rampage in Tucson, Arizona, in which six people were killed and thirteen injured, including U.S. Representative Gabrielle Giffords: "In the words of Job, 'when I looked for light, then came darkness'" (Job 30:26, NIV).

Advent, this season in the dark, is the church's time to support one another in finding courage to face and name the darkness, believing that the light is shining even there. Might we covenant together to use this Advent study as an opportunity to reconnect with the promise of God's everlasting faithfulness and eternal light? Can we grasp one another's hands tightly and hold one another in prayer? Can we trust, as did our ancestor Moses, that we will find God in the midst of the thick darkness? (Exodus 20:21). Shall we read the Holy Scripture together and see again how the saving light of God's new reign shines into the innermost corners and pockets of our hearts? Might we seek out the light as it comes to us from the tender mercy in the heart of our God, giving light to those who sit in darkness and in the shadow of death? (Luke 1:78-9)

The truth of our faith, the oft-hidden treasure of darkness, is that the birth of the Christ Child happens in the darkest dark of the night. In that night, God's love triumphs over the power of hopelessness and fear; and a special star shines so brightly that the whole of the night sky is brilliant with light. The world begins anew.

This is our faith; and when the light grows dim, we cling to it by the thinnest of threads, but cling we do. In times when we are wavering, the community of faith holds steady on our behalf. Week by week, we light the Advent candles, the candles that symbolize light shining in the darkness which the darkness can never put out (John 1). Their reassuring light is a testimony to our belief that God is present in the darkness. God, who formed light and created darkness (Isaiah 45:7), is sovereign of it all, alive in it all. God is with us in the darkness and walks with us through the valley of the shadow of death. God lights up our path, guides our feet, and gently invites us to lay aside our fear.

Even in the midst of our darkest days and nights, days of sorrow and nights of fear, God's promise is sure. We can cling to hope in the unshakeable hope of God's everlasting love for us. We can trust that even in the darkness, or rather, precisely in the darkness, God's light shines right where and when it is needed most and, indeed, "sometimes a light surprises!" (William Cowper, 1779).

And so, should you wake in the night and all the fears loom up, remember the starry messengers circling overhead and pray with the Psalmist these beautiful words written centuries ago, handed down by oral tradition, memorized by generation upon generation of the faithful:

You, O LORD, keep my lamp burning;
my God turns my darkness into light.
Psalm 18:28 (NIV)

In such moments, this God who provides comfort in the night is reassuringly close to our hearts. God becomes for us what one little girl called God—"a Bright Night Light," in Carolyn Bohler's book *God the What?: What our Metaphors for God Reveal About Our Beliefs in God).* In the darkness of your night, the light shines. Remember how the stars are meant to be seen and the surprising, wondrous message they bring.

In the words of poet Ann Weems:

Into this silent night
    as we make our weary way
we know not where,
    just when the night becomes its darkest
and we cannot see our path,
    just then
        is when angels rush in,
        their hands full of stars.

15

The Light in the Window

If you listen to radio, you've no doubt heard the old Motel 6 ad that had Tom Bodett promising weary travelers: "We'll leave the light on for you!" Don't we long to come home and find the light on?

Moravian Christians practice a unique way of welcoming the light each Advent and leaving a light on for the Christ Child. For generations, they have decorated their homes simply by lighting one candle in each window of the house. That's all. Theirs is an elegant and poignant witness to faith and hope. This custom comes from an old story that on Christmas Eve, the Christ Child carries bundles of evergreens and wanders all over the world. Those who long for his coming set a lighted candle in the window to welcome him into their home and hearts.

Each candle is a small light shining in the darkness, persisting in the darkness. Each welcomes God in Christ to this home on earth. Each signals belief in the power of every single candle to open up space in the darkness for a healing future made possible by the Advent of Christ.

The season of Advent brings the assurance that God is ready for us with the light on. All we have to do is do the same for God: Leave a light on in our heart and be ready to welcome in the light of Christ. Perhaps, based in this beautiful Moravian tradition and as part of our Advent study, each of us might resolve to light a candle in each "window" of our heart this Advent. On each windowsill of our soul, one candle will open the darkness just enough to create space for insight, for vision, for calm assurance and peace. It will signal our yearning for the Messiah, the light of the world shining in our darkness, to come to our hearts.

The light of God ever shines in the darkness. With the Psalmist, we can sing:

> *It is good to give thanks to the LORD,*
> *to sing praises to your name, O Most High;*
> *to declare your steadfast love in the morning,*
> *and your faithfulness by night.*
>
> ***Psalm 92:1-2***

Discussion Questions

1. What would help you slow down to let Advent be Advent for you this year?
2. What is your soul longing for in this season? What is your deepest need?
3. What are the places of darkness that are weighing heavily on you that you might bring to God in prayer?
4. What will be your heart's candle of healing and hope?
5. What images come to mind when you imagine God in a new way as our "Bright Night Light"?

Remember that if you wish companionship for this journey, beyond your Advent study group, seek out a pastor, a counselor, a 12-step group, a covenant group, or a Stephen Minister. Scripture assures us that we are not alone. There are those who will share their light with us.

Carols or Hymns for the Week

"It Came Upon the Midnight Clear"
"The Servant Song"

Focus for the Coming Week

The light of God comes—not only for each of us in a deeply personal way, but for all God's children everywhere. May the candles of our Advent wreath light up our hearts and SHINE! brightly over the whole of this earth!

The Light of the World

The people who walked in darkness
  have seen a great light;
those who lived in a land of deep darkness—
  on them light has shined.
You have multiplied the nation,
  you have increased its joy;
they rejoice before you
  as with joy at the harvest,
  as people exult when dividing plunder.
For the yoke of their burden,
  and the bar across their shoulders,
  the rod of their oppressor,
  you have broken as on the day of Midian.
For all the boots of the tramping warriors
  and all the garments rolled in blood
shall be burned as fuel for the fire.
For a child has been born for us,
  a son given to us;

authority rests upon his shoulders;
and he is named
Wonderful Counselor, Mighty God,
Everlasting Father, Prince of Peace.
His authority shall grow continually,
and there shall be endless peace
for the throne of David and his kingdom.
He will establish and uphold it
with justice and with righteousness
from this time onward and forevermore.
The zeal of the LORD of hosts will do this.

Isaiah 9:2-7

In Week 2 of our Advent study, we will explore how the light comes to bring light to all of God's children in every land.

Jesus Speaks Every Language

As Advent begins, our congregation has an annual tradition of putting up a big manger scene out in the center courtyard. Without fail, each year I witness little Christmas miracles down at the manger. One such miracle came by way of participants in a community group that meets at the church.

We host a weekly Swedish school. I had no idea that so many Swedes live in the Los Angeles area until this group came to us. They are young parents who want to pass on the culture and language to their children who are growing up here in the States.

One week just before Christmas, they had gathered for their annual St. Lucia celebration. The custom is based around the fourth-century Christian martyr Lucia, or Lucy, who comes at the time of the longest winter nights to chase away the dark and herald the promise of lengthening days and the coming of light. This custom is reenacted in homes and in Swedish gatherings each December 13. In Swedish tradition, a girl in each family dresses as Lucia, whose name means "light." She carries saffron breads and wears a crown of evergreen and lighted candles.

After the celebration one year, late in the afternoon as the sun was going down, I was walking past the crèche. I saw a little girl standing right by the manger. She had climbed inside to get close to the Baby Jesus, and she was just tall enough to look over the edge. She was leaning in close to his face and talking. And as I drew near, I could hear that she was speaking to the Baby Jesus in Swedish. He must surely have been responding to her, because she was carrying on quite a conversation with him. Standing patiently nearby was her dad, wisely knowing the importance of such a precious moment in the life and faith of his little daughter.

I chuckled to myself and thought it wonderful to know that Jesus speaks fluent Swedish. How fun it was to remember that even as a newborn Babe, he could communicate with a little girl, because she believed that he could and would. The scene I witnessed reminds us that God in Christ speaks all the languages of the human heart, hears us all, understands us all, comforts and receives us all.

[handwritten margin note: If we listen Jesus speaks to us in a language we can understand — even what he wants us to hear]

Where Darkness Covers the Land

Where I live in the city of Santa Monica, part of the huge Los Angeles metropolis comprised of people of many languages and cultures, the lights are on day and night. But there are still many places you can go on this earth and find that things are really dark at night. Others are not so fortunate as we. The bright, sparkly lights of our city stand in stark contrast to the darkness that still exists in many other parts of the world, places where electricity has still not yet arrived.

Sometimes while driving at night, I think back to roads I traveled in Madagascar on a mission trip. It is one of the poorest countries on earth. We would drive through the night to arrive at another school or mission hospital the next day. With no streetlights to show the way, seeing only by the light of our headlamps, we would bounce through the darkness on roads marred by deep potholes and ruts. Occasionally we would spot bits of light along the roadside. These were small fires burning in oil drums, with a few people gathered 'round for conversation as they journeyed between home and work. Others sought to sell a few fruits, gourds, or other items they had scavenged together to be able to buy rice for their family. The darkness of the night mirrored the darkness of the poverty and scarcity that burden that beautiful country.

New Testament scholar Marcus Borg writes that the Christmas story, taken as a whole, combines "what we often separate—namely religion and politics, spirituality and a passion for [the transformation] of this world," in *The First Christmas: What the Gospels Really Think About Jesus' Birth*.

The Christmas story holds together our hopes and fears and the hopes and fears of all God's people throughout the world. It leaves no barrier between the darkness of our hearts and the darkness of those conditions that limit people to less than the fullness of life. It dispels the shadows of death through which we each and all walk at times in our lives and the shadows of death, which hover over far too many of God's precious children. Upon it all will the light of Christ shine. But until that day dawns, the suffering of many of God's children is great.

Light in the Darkness

"In our troubled days it is good to have something outside our planet, something fine and distant for comfort." So said Annie Jump Cannon, an American astronomer who lived from 1863–1941. I should have liked to have known her, especially during the semester when I nearly failed my own college astrophysics course. Not easy stuff to get your head around. But Annie Jump Cannon did. This native of Dover, Delaware, graduated from Wellesley College in 1884, received her Master's in 1907, earned an honorary doctorate from the University of Delaware, and became the first person to receive an honorary degree from Oxford—a little over a century after the Wesleys were there—as well as an honorary doctorate from Wellesley College in 1925.

In 1896 Annie Jump Cannon was hired by Professor Edward Charles Pickering, director of the Harvard College Observatory, to catalogue variable stars and to classify the spectra of southern stars. The many women on staff were referred to as "computers" because they handled star classification and complex data reduction. You see, long before the electronic computer was invented in the 1940s, the word *computer* was applied to humans—people who did the highly skilled computations necessary for scientific work. Annie Jump Cannon was good at it. She was able to classify more than a quarter of a million stars, based on measurements of their spectra, with great speed and accuracy.

"In our troubled days it is good to have something outside our planet, something fine and distant for comfort," she said, looking to the stars for comfort and hope just before her death in 1941, as the United States prepared to enter the Second World War. What was the trouble and unrest of her time? There had been trouble in her early life, when, as a child, she became deaf as a result of serious illness. But there was trouble in the world too. She had lived through the period of Reconstruction following the Civil War; the Franco-Prussian War; the Battle of the Little Big Horn; the first Boer War; the assassination of President Garfield; a major hurricane in Galveston that killed 8,000 people; the first use of airplanes as offensive weapons; the sinking of the "Lusitania" passenger liner; the First World War; the Russian Revolution; the flu epidemic; the rise of Mussolini, Hitler, and Stalin; the Great Depression; and the Spanish Civil War. Through it all, Annie Jump Cannon persevered and found strength and assurance, looking to the light of the stars.

The Light of the World

Scripture gives us a variety of ways to hear the news that light shines in our darkness. The prophet Isaiah proclaims it:

> *The people who walked in darkness*
> *have seen a great light;*
> *those who lived in a land of deep darkness—*
> *on them light has shined....*

23

> *For a child has been born for us...*
> *and he is named*
> *Wonderful Counselor, Mighty God,*
> *Everlasting Father, Prince of Peace.*
> **Isaiah 9:2, 6**

The Gospel of John phrases it in poetic theological language: "The Word became flesh and dwelt among us" (1:14 *a*). "The light shines in the darkness and the darkness did not overcome it" (1:5).

In Luke's version of the story of Christ's birth, we hear the same promise described in the nitty-gritty real life version of how God came to live among us, in the story of Mary and Joseph, shepherds, angels, and a babe lying in a manger. The Gospel writer tells us that God came into our world as a real person in a very dark time. This story reads just like any news story about governors, power brokers, and various politicians. It's not much of a stretch for us to substitute the names of tyrants from today's headlines and realize that Scripture is talking about real time, real lives, and real struggles over life and death. Without a doubt, this is "Reality Gospel."

Some mornings, the news from that same real world is almost too much to bear in our time as when Mary and Joseph had to face it. There always seems to be more pain and suffering than we can hold and carry in our hearts and minds: wars and rumors of wars, death and betrayal, and natural disasters. In troubled days, as in the time when Jesus was born, as in the time when Annie Cannon worked as a human computer, as in the times in which we live, we, too, yearn to find the assurance of God's abiding presence and promise.

You know the places in your own life, your own heart, where you long for God's light to shine. You know the needs of loved ones, family, friends, co-workers, and all of the places that this light needs to shine for them. And you also know the places of darkness in our world that you would lift up to this light. Now, as at the time of Christ's birth, we cling to the hope that no matter how broken this world can sometimes be, how scary, how overwhelming, how confusing, or how disappointing, God's light shines in the darkness. And the darkness, Scripture assures us, has not overcome it. Still God chooses, out of love, to come and live among us, bringing light.

The amazing, life-changing news is that the coming of Christ is not simply about light; it is about light in the darkness. It is about light pushing back the darkness, light transforming the darkness by its luminous power. Christ comes as light coming into the darkness of our lives and of this world to cast out fear and to bring forth hope and new life. This is the light that is strong enough to show the way to peace amid violence and war. This is the light that can show the way to healing in every place of discord and brokenness. This is the light that can show the way to hope amid sadness and despair. This is the light of Christ—the light of peace, healing, and hope.

In Antananarivo, the capital of Madagascar, is a school for girls, run by the Women's Society of the Protestant Church. These girls are from the poorest of families, whose only prospects for earning money are found in lives of prostitution. The church's school gives them an alternative to that life. It teaches the girls to read and to learn crafts. Marketable skills such as sewing and embroidery offer them a way out of a life of misery and suffering. It is not an easy environment for the service of the devoted volunteers of the Women's Society. Some of the girls are already too broken to be able to succeed. Others are taken out of school by their parents, desperate for the immediate income they could be providing for the family. I asked one of the women how she found the strength to continue the work. "Christ would have me do no other," she said, in a voice of incredible strength and determination.

Thanks to the depth of her faith and her willingness to let Christ's light shine through her, light shines in the darkness of that place. It is not much brighter than the small lights by the side of the road at night. But by the power of Christ, it shines steadily and has enlightened the lives of many young girls and their families. The mission of the church throughout the world, in every place of brokenness, violence, poverty and fear, in every language across the globe, is the manifestation of Christ's light, for the true light that enlightens everyone, even now coming into the world (John 1).

The writer and poet Madeleine L'Engle put it this way, in her poem, "First Coming":

He did not wait till the world was ready,
till men and nations were at peace.
He came when the Heavens were unsteady,
and prisoners cried out for release.

He did not wait for the perfect time.
He came when the need was deep and great.
He dined with sinners in all their grime,
turned water into wine. He did not wait

till hearts were pure. In joy He came
to a tarnished world of sin and doubt.
To a world like ours, of anguished shame
He came, and his Light would not go out.

He came to a world which did not mesh,
to heal its tangles, shield its scorn.
In the mystery of the Word made Flesh
the Maker of the stars was born.

We cannot wait until the world is sane
to raise our songs with joyful voice,
for to share our grief, to *touch our pain,*
He came with Love: Rejoice! Rejoice!

The great German theologian Karl Barth insisted that the church approach faith and theology with the Bible in one hand and the newspaper in the other. In this second week of Advent, as we pray together for the coming of Christ's light into the world, try praying with the newspaper in one hand and the Bible in the other. Look beyond and through all the dark places of this world, through these troubled days, to find new hope in the coming of God's light. Lift up the hurting places of this world into the light of God's promised love and peace. Bear witness to the light—in every prayer for God's shalom, every act of healing, every word of hope shared, every act of justice and mercy offered, that the light may come for all God's children in every land.

war + homeless [handwritten]
hunger [handwritten]

Discussion Questions

1. What are some places of darkness in our world that trouble you?
2. What are ways you feel tempted to think that there's no hope for certain places or conditions?
3. Where do you find encouragement to persevere and "keep the faith"?
4. How do the Scriptures of this season renew your faith for peace and joy in the world?
5. Where do you long for the light to shine? *Peace* [handwritten]

Carols or Hymns for the Week

"O Holy Night"
"Star-Child," by Shirley Erena Murray and Carlton R. Young

Focus for the Coming Week

Where can we see the light shining? God's light shines bright in the lives of faithful people everywhere, but especially in the lives of young adults. May the candles of the Advent wreath renew our hope and open our eyes to see the light of God in the lives of others.

Shine a Light!

"Here's another way to put it: You're here to be light, bringing out the God-colors in the world. God is not a secret to be kept. We're going public with this, as public as a city on a hill. If I make you light-bearers, you don't think I'm going to hide you under a bucket, do you? I'm putting you on a light stand. Now that I've put you there on a hilltop, on a light stand—shine!"

Matthew 5:14-15a (THE MESSAGE)

In Week 3 of our Advent study, we ask where we see the light shining in this world of ours. We see it in the lives of all faithful people, but I'm firmly convinced that one place we see the light most clearly is in the lives of young adults.

Young Light-Bearers

Every year our congregation celebrates baptismal renewal on the Sunday shortly after Christmas, when we recall the baptism of Jesus. Scripture tells that as a young man, before he began his public ministry, Jesus himself was baptized by his cousin John, also a young man. On a day when many people were being baptized, Jesus, too, came and stepped up, presented himself, and made a life-changing commitment.

Our annual celebration of baptismal renewal is a time to remember that we are baptized, claimed by God to walk in the light through every day and every night of our living. But one year, the day was made extra special; for it was to be a day not just of renewal, but of baptism itself. We were celebrating the baptism of a young adult, a young man about the same age as Jesus himself at the time of his baptism.

We are blessed to baptize babies quite often in the life of our congregation. When a baby is baptized, of course, the parents and family pledge to raise the child in such a way that he or she will come to know the love and grace of Christ Jesus for himself or herself. But the baptism of an adult takes on added power and significance. When an adult comes forward, baptism is a sign of his or her own commitment, his or her choice, his or her decision to be part of Jesus' ministry of love and justice.

Jacob's decision to present himself for baptism and to publicly "put on Christ" became a witness and challenge for our whole congregation. His choice was deliberate, carefully considered, and deeply heartfelt, as was the choice of Jesus so long ago. The commitment he was making, as a young adult, gave us all the opportunity that day to consider again the choices we make about who we are and how we live. The baptism of that young adult pushed everyone to reflect anew on the ministry of Jesus himself and on our own commitments to live out our baptism, walking in the light of Christ. His witness helped everyone see with new eyes God's light shining through us and giving light to our path.

Perhaps I had to reach a certain age to finally realize that many of the major characters in the Jesus story play their best parts as young adults. Have you ever thought about the story this way? Mary and Joseph were young adults. Later, Jesus, as a young adult, seeks out his cousin John, another young adult, to be baptized. The disciples were young adults.

As with all young adults, there is an energy in how they live, a frankness, a willingness to commit everything for a goal, an ideal, a deeply held belief. They seek spirituality, truth, and authenticity. They are searching for hope and direction as they strive to own their faith in an often skeptical world.

Don't you know young adults who are full of questions, including the big life-questions of vocation, relationships, and faith? They are passionate about seeing God more clearly as their companion in the adventure of life. In the process of addressing their questions, lives are changed, faith grows deeper, and light shines.

Jim Wallis of the Sojourners community in Washington, D.C., describes why he includes teaching stints at Harvard in his busy schedule each year. Having taught in the Divinity School's Center for the Study of Values in Public Life and the Kennedy School of Government in areas of "religion and public life," he wrote that he was amazed at large numbers of religious and "secular" students who packed lecture halls "hungry to discuss the connections between politics and moral values.... I could feel myself moved by the students," he said. "They are the next generation ... and the focus for so many of [them] is how to put their faith into action in a world in desperate need of both justice and hope."

Let Your Light Shine

A couple years ago, returning to the U.S. after a mission trip to Mozambique, I was struck by the many young adults I met at the various airports in Africa where we made connections on the return journey. Some were church-based, others were there at their own initiative. Several, with designs on being teachers, had come to tutor kids. One, studying to be a water sanitation engineer, had come to build wells for safe drinking water. Another, aspiring to be a doctor, had come to distribute insecticide-treated anti-malarial bed nets. They had all chosen to take a year or more out of school, to put their beliefs into practice. They had all chosen to let their light shine to make the lives of others a bit brighter, a bit healthier, a bit more hopeful.

One of the young women on our trip is a wonderful witness to how God's light shines in the lives of young adults eager to bring light, justice, and hope to the world as she lives out the light of her baptism. Beth teaches second grade, works as a camp counselor and environmental educator at an outdoor education center and traditional Appalachian farm that teaches people how to live off the land in a sustainable way, and tutors after school twice a week. She is active in her home church and in United Methodist Women and is working to get a young adult ministry going.

Her first mission trip came during college. She went to Mexico to work at an orphanage, an experience that opened her eyes and ignited her passion for international mission. Teaching English at an orphanage school in Tanzania for a month inspired her to get her Master's degree in TESOL (Teaching English to Speakers of Other Languages). Having now been to Mozambique several times, she is eager to get her whole church excited about mission, particularly international mission, which previously had not been her focus. She will be taking a second group from her church to Mozambique in 2012. God's light shines brightly in the life of this remarkable young woman. Through her, it shines into her home church and into the lives of the many people she has met and served. She is on a path, illuminated by God's Word, to become the person God has created her to be and to let her light shine.

With young adults, we can explore together our vocational and faith questions, looking as we all are for light in our darkness. As American writer and theologian Frederick Buechner puts it: "The place where God calls you to is the place where your deep gladness and the world's deep hunger meet." Walking in the light of Christ, we may find ourselves at that holy intersection with the young adults of the Christmas story and the young adults of our congregations and communities. With Mary, Elizabeth, Joseph, John, Jacob, and Beth, light-bearers all, we may find the light of Christ shining bright in ways we might never have imagined. God wants us all to SHINE!

We Are Children of the Light

All baptized Christians are children of light. The early church called baptism by the Greek name *photismos,* which means "enlightening" or "illumination." When we put on Christ in our baptism, we become radiant with his light. We each become part of the light of Christ's glory and truth; and we set out, through our lives, to share that light with others. The energy of light is transformed within us into the generative energy of love and service.

This radiant energy is especially apparent in young adults whose faith is forming and growing and questioning. St. Irenaeus, one of the early church fathers, said that "the glory of God is man [and woman] fully alive." God wants us to believe, to become, to grow into the fullness of who God has created us to be.

One window into the faith journey and questing spirituality of young adults can be found at a place called Taizé, in France, where thousands are seeking community and finding deeper faith. The Taizé community is an ecumenical monastic order with a strong commitment to peace, justice, and reconciliation through worship and prayer. It has become one of the world's most important sites of Christian pilgrimage, every summer drawing upwards of 6,000 people, mostly young adults, who come from more than fifty countries and from every continent.

They come to find a place to explore all their questions of faith, vocation, and identity in a joyous, welcoming Christian community. They seem to be drawn by the hospitality, the prayer, and the light. The style of worship at Taizé is simple and meditative. It is based around silence, prayer, the singing of simple chants, and the lighting of candles. The richly diverse and ecumenical congregation gathers in silence and sings in their many languages. As candles are lit and light floods the chapel, illuminating all who are present, they sing some of the beautiful Taizé chants that celebrate light:

> Stay with me, Lord Jesus Christ,
> night will soon fall.
> Stay with me, Lord Jesus Christ,
> light in our darkness."

> Our darkness is never darkness in your sight:
> the deepest night is clear as the daylight.

The many young adults who flock to Taizé are representative of the searching, committed faith that formed the Christian church at its beginnings and will lead it into a future of hope. How might we create a similar spiritual home for them in our own congregations?

"Elizabeth" Someone This Advent

At the same time, young adults are often eager for support and mentoring. We see it in the story of Jesus' birth. As a young woman, Mary faced a challenge as she carried the baby to be born Child of God. She sought to be faithful and righteous. She strove to do the right thing by Joseph. But surely she had questions. She was uncertain and needed help to sort it all out. After being visited by the angel Gabriel, she immediately journeyed to the home of her cousin Elizabeth. She needed a listening ear, an understanding heart, a loving mentor. Quickly making the journey from Nazareth to the hill country of Judea, a journey of some eighty to one hundred miles, she entered the house; and her cousin heard her greeting. Elizabeth was overcome by God's presence. The Scriptures say that she was filled with the Holy Spirit. Elizabeth blessed Mary, reassured her, and validated her faith. Elizabeth became a spiritual mentor to Mary. She called out Mary's gifts. She supported her intuition and her choice. She helped Mary become the person God was calling her to be.

All of us adults, young and old, sometimes need the support and mentoring of an Elizabeth to help us see ourselves in God's light. It's not easy work for most of us. We have doubts, don't we? We tend to undervalue our own gifts. We rarely trust our own great potential. Fortunately, we don't make this journey alone, but in the beauty and the power of Christian community. When it is hard for us to see our own gifts, when it is difficult to claim our potential, we need an Elizabeth in our lives.

One of the young adult members of our congregation is passionate about being a "big sister" to a young woman who has grown up with much less than she—less family support, less opportunity, less confidence, and lower self-esteem. Our member spends time with her "little sister" each week. They talk, they go shopping, they go to sports events and concerts and movies. They talk some more. An amazing bond has formed. And through it all, this one young woman has been "Elizabethed" by her big sister, her spiritual mentor, her loving friend, into believing that her life has all of the potential for a beautiful future.

Traditionally, in the third week of Advent, we light the pink candle, Mary's candle, of the Advent wreath. As you do so this year, during Week 3 of our Advent study, think about the role her cousin Elizabeth played in supporting her to become the person God had created her to be. Consider the gifts God has also given you. Take some time too to call out the gifts of others who are close to you. Let Advent be a time of "Elizabething" one another in Christian love, drawing out one another's gifts, deepening the bonds of Christian love and fellowship within the beloved community.

In our congregation, as part of each baptism, we light a baptismal candle from the paschal candle and give it to the family or to the person being baptized. It symbolizes the light of Christ they now carry within. None of us can know how and when we will be called upon to let our light shine or what darkness it may illumine for another. We cannot know in advance what dark places of the human heart or of this world it might open, what joy it will bring, what comfort or hope. We can only be ready and ever willing to share with others the light we have received.

Especially this year, as we let the story of Christ's birth shed light onto our lives, make space for the young adults to shine brightly. Support them, mentor them, and let their passion for God's future renew hope within your congregation and community. Dr. Lovett H. Weems, Jr., Distinguished Professor of Church Leadership and Director of the Lewis Center for Church Leadership at Wesley Theological Seminary, in Washington, D.C., points out that "there is no future for United Methodism in America unless we can figure how to reach more people, younger people and more diverse people."

If we're ever tempted to be fearful about the church and its future, remember the young adults who set it in motion and whose commitment and joy can light up the church, which is too often stuck in its ways and fearful of its future. As one young adult commentator, Shane Claiborne, noting that Jesus was a young adult in mission and ministry, put it: "[The church] suffer[s] most deeply from a paralysis of imagination. You can't miss that in Jesus—he had the imagination to point us toward something more" (from *Devo'Zine* magazine, Sept. 4, 2009).

Discussion Questions

1. How might God be calling you to let your light shine this Advent?
2. Can you describe a young adult whose faith is an inspiration to your own?
3. What might your congregation do to encourage the ministry and spiritual formation of young adults?
4. How might you "Elizabeth" or mentor a young adult?
5. What "something more" can you envision for your congregation?

Carols or Hymns for the Week

"I Want to Walk as a Child of the Light"
"Gather Us In"

Focus for the Coming Week

The horizon glows with the Advent of Christ's coming. Can you see the light beginning to shine? Can you imagine a future with hope? May the light of our Advent candles open our eyes to God's promise of life made new.

The Horizon Is Bright

I wait for the LORD, my soul waits,
and in his word I hope;
my soul waits for the Lord
more than those who watch for the morning,
more than those who watch for the morning.

O Israel, hope in the LORD!
For with the LORD there is steadfast love,
and with him is great power to redeem.

Psalm 130:5-7

In Week 4 of our Advent study, we will look for the light of God making bright God's promised future of hope and peace.

Watch and Wait

As we move into the fourth week of Advent, our eyes are drawn into the future. As we prepare for the birth of the Christ Child, we are reminded of God's plan for the whole creation. In the fullness of time will be a new birth of all that is, a new heaven and a new earth. Our lives, with all their ups and downs, joys and sorrows; and this world, with its aches and pains, its hurting and broken places—are all held in the trajectory of a loving and gracious God who yearns for our wholeness, our salvation and our peace.

Advent summons us to the wellsprings of our faith and hope. God has another vision for this earth, a vision in which none shall live afraid, in which the darkness holds more treasure than terror. We light four candles and still we watch and wait.

The beloved Catholic writer and pastor Henri Nouwen once wrote: "A waiting person is a patient person. The word *patience* means the willingness to stay where we are and live the situation out to the full in the belief that something hidden there will manifest itself to us." As we move together into the fourth week of Advent, we are waiting and watching—waiting for all the "treasures of the dark" to be revealed, waiting for the redemptive promises of God to be manifest, and watching the night sky to see the first signs of morning light.

But we're not particularly patient people, are we? We are into instant everything—instant messaging, instant food, instant gratification. One of my favorite little note cards was given me by a parishioner some years ago as we were working our way through some changes at the church. It reads: "Lord, give me patience. *AND GIVE IT TO ME NOW!*" Don't you feel exactly the same way sometimes?

It's not easy to be patient and wait until we can see clearly. A murky human-made smog of dreams deferred, of violence, confusion, change, fear, and frustration can sting our eyes and sometimes blur even what is closest to us. Where God would bring light, we are often stuck in the darkness of ignorance and fear.

In the fourth week, the season of Advent continues to invite us to set aside our impatience and our sarcasm. It offers us the hope-filled perspective of waiting and watching. Its promise is that our waiting will not be in vain, for what God promises, God will do. Amid Advent's "treasures of darkness" is the conviction that our eyes and the eyes of our heart will see a horizon becoming bright with joy and with hope. To us the Epistle speaks: "You will do well to be attentive to this as to a lamp shining in a dark place, until the day dawns and the morning star rises in your hearts" (2 Peter 1:19*b*).

Our Advent worship represents this in a beautiful way. Over the last several years, the larger church has been moving away from the penitential reddish-purple color, long associated with Advent paraments for worship, leaving that for the Lenten season. In more and more congregations, we now mark the season of Advent with its own color. It is a deep, dark blue, a color brimming with anticipation and expectation. We might describe it as the color of the star-filled sky, the night sky just before dawn, a very dark, blackish-blue, glowing with light about to be revealed, pregnant with light, bursting with possibility, this blue heralding the birth of our Savior, Jesus Christ. It is the color of a darkness just ready to brim over with light, the light of a new day, new promise, new hope, new beginnings. It's the light we perceive before we see it, because we have longed for it and yearned for it to come into our darkness.

As the light of Advent begins to lend a faint luminescent glow to the deep darkness of our night's sky, awareness begins to dawn in us that newness of life is possible after all in our lives and in this world. Advent points us to the future, God's future; and in it, our own begins to come into view as well. God has so much more in store for us than we can even imagine.

Three Times More Everything

What do we see when we look at the night sky? How do we know what's really out there? What if we're missing a lot? How do we measure the full potential of all that God, the Maker of the stars, has created and is still creating?

It's easy to think that we are seeing the stars as they were meant to be seen, but we may well be still seeing them in the same way Annie Jump Cannon saw and counted them. An astonishing discovery made recently by astronomers opens up vast new possibilities. Last December, scientists from Yale and the Harvard-Smithsonian Center for Astrophysics, in Cambridge, reported that the number of stars in the night sky has been seriously undercounted. They determined that there are most likely three times as many stars out there as had been thought. Three times as many stars! It seems that they had not counted all of the dwarf-like stars in relation to the big sun-like stars, and they had not realized that galaxies come in many sizes and shapes—not just in the spiral-like pattern of our own Milky Way. Scientists had apparently been approaching the sky with flawed assumptions about what's up there and how it works. Now, new research has opened up vast new understandings of just what the sky contains.

Three times as many stars. I'd always thought that the number of stars was infinite, so ... three times infinite, ... what can that be? So many more than we ever thought. Stars upon stars upon stars. Commenting on this, a researcher at Cal Tech said that this new report reminds us "how fragile our knowledge of the universe is."

We think that we've got it nailed down, but there's so much more. The night sky has become even more luminous, more mysterious, more vast. It's awesome. And if there are three times as many stars, perhaps there is three times as much beauty. Three times as much love. Three times as much hope. Three times as much grace and salvation.

Such is the vastness of the promised Reign of God. If we hold on to too small a notion of God, too fragile an experience of God, with flawed assumptions about God and God's intent for this world, Advent invites us to let all of that go and begin anew. If we harbor the resignation of feeling that nothing much is ever going to change in this life, Advent challenges us to reframe our assumptions. In Advent, God's Word reminds us that we have been looking at it all wrong. There is so much more. There is always so much more—at least three times three times three times more.

Our God has so very much in store for us and for this weary world, much, much more than we let ourselves imagine. God longs for the windows of our hearts to be lit in welcome, for our eyes to see, for us not to be afraid in the dark. God encourages us to delight in all of the unexpected treasures of both the night and of the dawning light. Our God is eager to show us the stars as they are truly meant to be—

another way to live, another way to think, another way to believe and pray, always pointing us toward another world to imagine, the world as God intends it. This is what Advent is for, after all, to teach us how to watch and wait, to trust the promise, and to remind us how to live fully and faithfully as we walk in the light.

By the Light of This Light

Do you ever wonder or worry about what the future will be like? Futurist John Scharr said, "The future is not a result of choices among alternative paths offered by the present, but a place that is created— created first in the mind and will, created next in activity. The future is not some place we are going to, but one we are creating."

As Christ's baptized disciples, filled with light, we are a part of creating that future with God, creating a new future for this world, a future with possibilities as yet undreamed, a future with hope. With every choice we make and every action we take, every choice for life over death and blessing over curse, we are creating a new future. Every time we reach out when others ask, "Why bother?" and every time we refuse to accept that a door is closed or a fate is sealed, we are choosing to be part of what is called in Hebrew, *tikkun*, the work of mending, repairing and transforming the world.

The light of God opens our eyes to a whole new sky, a whole new world, a new heaven and a new earth. In the promised Reign of our God, for which we wait and watch all through these weeks of Advent, the blind will see, the people will live in peace and unafraid. In the promised Reign of our God, the lion and the lamb will lie down together, we will walk unharmed through the valley of the shadow of death, and the glory of the Lord will be revealed. And as we wait and watch, things start to change right before our very eyes. The stars increase. The light glows brighter. The world changes, lit by the fire of love.

There is a Jewish story based on the Talmud about the ending of night and the coming of the dawn. A rabbi asks his students: "How can we know when the night has ended and the day has begun?"

✱ A student answers: "You know the night has ended when you can distinguish a goat from a sheep." A second suggests: "You know the night has ended when you can distinguish between an olive tree and a fig tree."

The rabbi shakes his head. Immediately, the disciples begin to argue with one another. "Answer your own question, rabbi, for we cannot think of another response."

Then he speaks. "When you look into the eyes of another human being and see a brother or a sister, then you will know that the night has ended and the day has begun."

A whole new world is being born in the light of God's love. These things don't necessarily dawn on us suddenly or all at once. The light dawns slowly, almost imperceptibly. All through Advent, we have been practicing the spiritual discipline of seeing the earth in the light of God's intention for it, full of love and hope. As we wait and watch for the coming of the Messiah, we practice seeing with the eyes of the prophets and the evangelists. We train our hearts to begin to see that day of peace, the renewal of creation, the wholeness of life restored for all. Like artists of a new day, creating the future with God, we begin to sketch out a picture in our mind's eye of that day when all people will be drawn together in love and none will live afraid.

It takes time and patience and perseverance to see in the dark. Mary had to ponder all of these things in her heart a great while. Jesus' closest disciples—Peter, James, and John—and the other disciples were frequently in the dark about their new Messiah and his Reign. Gradually their eyes were opened and they began to change, little by little. They began to see the world as it is and to see the light of Christ shining through it all. They began to realize that there's much more than they had seen—maybe three times more or three times three times three more! And in that light, like them we, too, will begin to see ourselves empowered in our own sphere of influence, to make it more beautiful, more just and more whole.

Aren't we called to see ourselves and the world with new eyes? It's as if we need to put on a pair of "Advent glasses" to bring into focus all of the new possibilities made visible in the light of Christ. Heaven knows, we need one another and we need faith to keep these special "Advent glasses" on. Theologian Reinhold Niebuhr wrote: "Nothing worth doing is completed in our lifetime; therefore we must be saved by hope. Nothing true or beautiful makes complete sense in any immediate context of history; therefore we must be saved by faith. Nothing we do, however virtuous, can be accomplished alone; therefore, we are saved by love."

Be the Hope!

With the coming of the light of Christ, we are saved by hope, saved by faith and saved by love. As a new church year begins with Advent, we, too, are new with the light of Christ shining from deep within us. We can trust that God is doing a new thing among us, that God is already causing the light to shine. This we see in the light of our Advent hope, three times three times three times more than we ever imagined possible.

There's a big banner hanging off the railing above our center courtyard. It reads "Be the Hope." We had it made right after Hurricane Katrina, when the United Methodist Committee on Relief launched the "Be the Hope" ad campaign. They produced flyers and bulletin inserts, put a full-page ad in *USA Today*. They were telling the story of how The United Methodist Church responds to people in need with money, with work teams, with supplies, with prayer, and with love—all tangible expressions of the overall theme to "Be the Hope." In the years that followed, as our congregation sent adult and youth work teams to New Orleans, "Be the Hope" became our unofficial motto. The banner went up and has stayed up.

My friend, the pastor at St. Paul's Lutheran Church, around the corner, told me that he took his confirmation class on a faith walk around our neighborhood. They looked at houses and trees, and homeless people in the park. They looked at old people and kids and mothers with babies in strollers. They looked at churches, including ours. He said that when they got back to St. Paul's to reflect on their experience, the kids said that their favorite thing on the whole faith walk was our banner—"Be the Hope!" Our banner was what had caught their imagination. They loved it. "What does it mean?" they asked. "What's it there for?"

That led into an hour-long discussion about what "be the hope" might mean for them as part of their confirmation journey, as part of their sorting out what it means to be a baptized disciple of Jesus Christ. It applies to us all, doesn't it? In the light of Christ, we are empowered to "be the hope" as we serve in this world and as, with God, we create the future.

Adventure With Christ

As our Advent study draws to a close, the light of Christ shines in us in new ways now, illuminating us to "be the hope" in personal circumstances, in our communities and world, for the young adults we meet, and in the future that we are creating with God.

The word itself, *advent,* means the "coming" or "arrival" of something important. To the church, it means the coming of our Lord and Savior, Jesus Christ. It is from the same root as our word *adventure,* which literally means "an undertaking or experience involving taking a risk, daring, proceedinging despite the risks." This is a great definition of the Christian life as we walk in the light of Christ.

John Wesley described it this way: He called his Methodist people to journey and adventure with Christ. "Cast yourselves upon his righteousness as that which shall bring you to God....If you stay where you are, you perish," Wesley said. "Christ offers [and] if you will venture with him, he will bring you home and he will bring you to God."

Wesley posed this challenge and invitation to the people called Methodist in the "Directions for Renewing Our Covenant With God" in his Covenant Service of 1780. Some congregations still today mark the New Year with Wesley's Watch Night Service, a service of covenant renewal. Wouldn't that be a wonderful way to wrap up this Advent study and begin a new year together?

Adventure with Christ in this new year. Light the lamp. Shine brightly with Christ's light. Be the hope! Discover healing for your own hurts and brokenness. Find new energy for living and serving. Witness to all of the possibilities of the shalom of the world. Reimagine life in all the rainbowed possibilities of the full spectrum of God's light. "Elizabeth" someone into the fullness of their God-given potential. Live into a future bright with promise, illuminated by the mystery and the glory and the assurance of God.

> *"Arise, shine; for your light has come,*
>
> *and the glory of the LORD has risen upon you."*
>
> **Isaiah 60:1**

SHINE!

Discussion Questions

1. Where do you see signs of light breaking into the darkness of the world?
2. In what ways do you feel like you are patiently waiting or already shining?
3. What are the signs of the new Reign of God already present in our communities?
4. How do you see your congregation or the larger church "being the hope?"
5. How might you "adventure with Christ" in this New Year?

Carols or Hymns for the Week

"God Who Stretched the Spangled Heavens"
"Bring Forth the Kingdom"

Closing Prayer

Ever-creating, ever-revealing, ever-sustaining God, be with us in our darkness and cause us to shine forth in the brightness of your light. Reveal your glory to your people and let it shine bright within each of us. May your light keep us brave, strong, and focused. Make us patient to persevere, keeping the light on in the windows of our heart.

May the fullness of who you create us to be shine forth. Renew our hope for our own lives and for our world. May your light bring life to all of your people. Shine in us and let us shine!

Maranatha! Come, Lord Jesus, come. Amen.